AF422771

Mantra & Jam

Larry Levy

Independently Published.

First Edition 2022

Acknowledgments

Special thanks to: Cat, Clarinda Harriss, and Rosanne Horowitz.

Thanks to: The Ivy (Emily, Hannah, Rhea), Mickey, and everyone who has read, commented, and supported me through the past five books.

Contents

Mantra & Jam

Mantra

I smile
        because a minor key
opens locked doors.

Adoption

I walk to Germany to retrace her footsteps.
Grandmother serves me coffee-milk in mother's mug.
Their faces belong to me.
I am blond and blue.
I eat lovers and
I spit them out.

Through the bulrushes swaddling across the Rhine,
I search for my Aryan mother.
"Sephora became a heroin addict --
a slave to her master.
She left the Fatherland shackled to her misfortunes."

My stepbrother and I meet.
Biology brings us to our nihilistic knees.
She has done this before.
Pulled wings from butterflies
and repressed them between parchment.

He looks like me.
Upon reflection, like her.
Narcissus in blue jeans.

She kept the receipts.
Before chemicals removed her stain
mother disposed of us properly.

<u>Underneath The Shingles</u>

The ritual of family and red-brick homes
    of suburban pride and quarter acres
    with 2.5 children, crew cuts like manicured lawns,
The spit and shine
    of boots that stomp to the march
    "Hut! Hut! Hut!" - off to work again and yet again
    while wives preheat their mortgaged bearded jewels,
The mothers
    yes-men who love their sons
    give them the milk and D.N.A. of freedom,
The fathers
    pollen and brimstone on a merry-go-round
    in offices on couches with secretaries
    praying between the golden calves and undergarments,
    the biodegradable substitute for wives,
The sons
    stoners and acid lickers from Woodstock to Eden
    tribesmen of the experimental
    locked in a duel with reality,
The daughters
    with perfect teeth and smiles
    miles and miles of Pepsodent smiles who
    entertain boys in bathrooms
    while fathers dream of virgins slow dancing at weddings,
The grand ma-mas
    Maxwell House philosophers
    fibromyalgia poets and gurus of the neurotic
    weight-watched and valium'd
    into upper-middle-class submission,

The grand poohbahs
    encyclopedias on arthritic legs who
    once swam and copulated in the fearful brine
    of tradition and repetition.

Lost Girl

You ate through the gingerbread house
after drunk found its way into your bedroom.
Your mother made cookies to calm her nerves.

My father christened you 'Blue, the blind
step-child of complicity."
I knew you from across the way.

You showed me how easily boys' bruise
after you caught me, eye-balling
through a crack in the bathroom door.

Then you scratched my records.
"A dirty worn-out needle deforms the groove!"
Retribution for what you had lost.

I softened drawings
by rubbing my fingers across the page.
You blotted out the sun.

Seurat had a flair for the incompatible.
Harmony from the contrary, calm through balance.
Our friendship looked better from a distance.

Sunday Afternoon on the Island of La Grande Jatte.
You are the little girl in orange
skipping off into the trees.

Ghost

I see my father's face
   behind a web of winter trees.
Tent-poles elbow the sky
   holding his weary head
in disbelief.

He is gone
   along with the enchantment
of song I took for granted.

On Easter Sunday he said to me:

"I am drunk, though I do not drink.
   I am full, though I do not eat.
I may sit or rise, but am not bound by either.
   I have no fear, my family will forgive me."

And then he walked outside and disappeared.

First Love

Sons idolize mothers.
Mothers slumber in deceit.
Lovers kill dreams while the sons are asleep.
The dagger within penetrates deep
and leaves an open grave
for all the women who need to be saved
by me.

<u>Jam</u>

I drove down the corridor of dark anxious as a cat,
jungle and wild to the Holiday Inn, my old paint
headlong after the great Slavic goddess took off
her clothes for money, rubles thrown like confetti
to a celebrated contortionist writhing on a blanket,

Socialist prophet lending out his girl on the corner
of Baltimore and Gay before our dinner with Italians,
table for two in the den where Caesar served Natasha lobster
and corkscrew pasta to every marinara blooded male
watching my pride wind around tables on stilts,

Despised by every knife bearing woman cutting into her
veal scallopini wondering how slender slipped into faux
skin, silver threads well above the knee no bra no panties
and casual disregard for any non-pro suburbanite who sold
too cheap,

Past the chefs to the water closet to fire up, dull the senses,
beat me to the ball; back down the runway a fixed
Modigliani, heavy head, chin down, somnambulist eyes,
no appetite, the check-and-wink from waiter and maître d',

A whistle for the red chariot to steer us to our denouncement,
metal wheel, metal dash, metal tape in the Teac,
Tchaikovsky's Piano Concerto in b-flat minor an illustrious
key guaranteed to open locked doors for two hours,
80 bucks, clean sheets, T.V. and bathroom, "no I don't listen
to classical music, I'm a stripper,"

The harmony of hashish to lower my blood pressure,
lusciousness on a plate breathing heavy in a minor key,
four finger-chords going down the keyboard to wherever
inspiration and my imagination take me,

Back to the club where I first had her
seated on a park bench behind porous curtains, "now sit up
straight son or you'll get a humpback" the thrill of sex in a
booth inside a gorgeous girl with only a three-song window --
major key stuff -- that took a week of dreams to complete,

Fingering the dark keys, harping on strings, strung-out and
alive by the grace of the needle that stuck her before I did,
before Dostoevsky did, his Netochka, my Natasha, away from
the mirrors foreshadowing her unveiled dance driving me and
my wallet to romanticize heaven,

The mechanical undertaker crowned by the folly of youth and
small-headed desires, testing negative a week later, "you mean,
you paid for this?" the obvious outcome for hoping to unlock
the mystery of the universal womb in the filth of the underbelly
bedeviled by melancholy in a minor key.

Mantra

I smile
      because music is the bridge
from passion to enlightenment.

Prelude

Softness pulls the moist from lips.
The subterranean delve.
My silhouette on yours.

Thunder.
Chords trickle down.
Dissolution.

Sunlight dancing in the morning jubilee.
Curtains sheer, I kiss you down.
Down the corridor that left you wide.

Mist of strange on shore's lost comfort.
Wash clean the spoils.
Yesterday's squandered bounty.

Dreams rejuvenate our pulse.
Harmonies from an intemperate breeze.
Cool waves of pitch.

I count the encumbrances.
Fragments. Whispers. Hunger.
Between our lumbering breath.

The song sings deep in what was and must be again.
Innocence tricked us in safe slumber.

Star

Rhyme is holding hands.
Playing chords in major keys.
Eternity at our fingertips.

Sometimes I choose to rhyme.
Sometimes not.
Songwriting brings us together
and makes us no money.

If comeliness becomes your ticket
I will be miserable jealous lost.
Flush beats a straight every time.

Submission to your talent.
Queen to King four.
Checkmate.

In grade school everything was linear.
We drew timelines ahead of the curve.
Parallels not parabolas.

There is no justice in love.
Fair play runs afoul.
I eat more chicken than Jim Morrison.

I stink, you stink
yet we put our mouths where they
probably should not go.

Better to enunciate clearly
than speak in broken sentences
under the weight of a dispassionate lover.

Next

When your lips carry my voice --
a melody built from the body of bones --
the lyrical accomplices feel sorrow
every time the DJ spins.

A mixture of ecstasy and affectation
the combination unlocks
the lonely in your eyes.

I velvet the trace of fingers
blurring obscurity into insignificance
the invisible girl hidden in the shadows.

All is fair past the turnstiles of bars and clubs
the perfidy and tumult
strangers swallow in the dark.

I listen to you breathe fear into pitch
seduced by the magic of beat
washing clean bad choices.

I beer my way through the haze
stupefy and stumble from
every record that spurns my attention.

Broken sentences toil without reward.
I cry as a boy for the man who
loves without words.

Fade, fade, fade, gray, gray, winter night
into the storm of diminished expectations
my collar turned up into the oh well of rejection.

Mademoiselle in Shades of Relief

There is no slack in how she holds herself
    nor flabbiness in her intention.
I contemplate the art of painting
    to make her mine.

But I am unworthy in my efforts
    to capture the essence of her face.
With her back toward me,
    I feel the abstract quality of music more fitting.

I open the key-lid to my piano,
    and improvise a poem of sorrow and regret.
Black keys abscond my fingers.
    I struggle with the same anonymity as hers.

I am in the presence of a higher being,
    so lovely the voicing.
Between the arpeggios and fallen chords
    I become Debussy.

II.

I am grateful for the gift of
    serenity and quiet charm.
My desire to paint behind her back
    with leading tones of pink and blue.

Connected only to Mademoiselle,
    my fingers cascade down the gentle slope of melody.
Her hair coils to spring
    from the harmony of newly spun glissandos.

I remain drawn to the impulses of a young woman,
        fifty-four measures of suggestion.
A mere three-and-a-half minutes
        of beauty seeking admiration.

III.

She was lovelier than a bowl of fruit
        or flowers to Renoir.
But she died a still life
        when my fingers levitated from the keys.

These words will have to do.

<u>Passion by Example</u>

Plato thought mathematics and music were
the building blocks for the entire universe.

Goethe the great German poet stated:
"Music is liquid architecture.
Architecture is frozen music."

Albert Einstein who adored Goethe famously said:
"My sense of God is my sense of wonder about the universe."
He loved the architectural structure of Bach's music and
despised Wagner for his lack of it.

The piccolo trumpet solo in The Beatles' "Penny Lane"
inspired by Bach's Second Brandenburg Concerto:
"Blackbird" by Bach's Bourree in E minor.

I had my first religious experience
when Virgil Fox performed Bach's,
Toccata and Fugue in D. Minor
for heavy organ at the Lyric Theater.

The next day I bought my first classical record,
Bach: Brandenburg Concerti Nos. 4, 5, and 6
performed by the Wurttenberg Chamber Orchestra.

My second transformation came when I unwrapped
my purchase and heard the harpsichordist Martin Galling
play the solo in Bach's Fifth Brandenburg Concerto.

Contrapuntal music of which Bach excelled
is when two independent melodic lines
work in harmony with each other.

This is what I learned from love.

Jam

Like the time in biology class when I stealthily read *Creem*
        Magazine and learned Ringo & Ginger were
        the best drummers instead of dissecting starfish,

Like the time I hit the stage with mates and beard
        and nose and glasses in front of the
        entire school laughing,

Like the time I later discovered the consequence of
        acoustics where tile and cement were
        the true keepers of time,

Like the time I rolled through the silver sparkle gates of
        Peabody hair akimbo and passed the audition
        on condition I held my sticks properly,

Like the time during a sacred jam when the guitar player
        turned and yelled at me to stop jazzing
        and I immediately quit lessons,

Like the time I gutted-out from going to California
        because middle-class security found me
        too fearful to pursue the dream,

Like the time I played on a rubber pad on the balcony
        of my girlfriend's apartment to regain the
        skills I had lost,

Like the time I hauled my drums to Annapolis because
        the music was cool, new, fresh, and the
        singer had the voice of an angel,

Like the time when I had become ensnared with
                a pretty face who between sets abused me
                into the bowels of the basement to drink alone,

Like the time I ran off stage in one-hundred-degree heat
                and saturated a cinder block in the alley
                certain I was going to die,

Like the time in Toronto when our zoftig promoter
                wanted to rock 'n roll and I chose to get
                a tattoo instead,

and the time after that and after that and after that when
organized chaos kept me grounded structured sane gifted
and lifted to the stars there and aware in my own head
nirvana in the basement in clubs in bars in studios
beating me senseless and deaf to the mundane world below
passing through this life with the knowledge and vibe and
pulse of eternity.

Mantra

I smile
      because girls with crosses
bear the spike of ecstasy.

Smack!

I gave my money to this skinny chick.
She whipped me with her defiance.

We all know the type.
Always in trouble, never caught.

Smoked cigs, drank, no food, no sleep,
crucifix pointing down between her breasts.

Teenage ass never had daddy's hand across it --
Smack! The one thing she needed most.

Her Highness, Miss Tightwad!
Comptroller of both pouch and purse.

Thin as a dime between the legs
spread 'em easy for a man who despised her.

Married young, divorced with a black eye
got the Camaro in the settlement.

Took her clothes off on a downtown stage
and preyed on small denominations like me.

Got tired of throwing her singles
so I signed my paycheck over to her.

Had her once or twice on an unmade bed
with her kid sleeping in another room.

Moved in with a dude who
sold her silver and gold to a hock shop.

I got wise eventually
and pursued my pleasure uptown.

Resolute

Bobbing up and down.
In a barrel, words hibernate.
We cling to the margins.

To comprehend being in a flash
we must bottle the fire that finds us
overwhelmed by the rain.

You towel me off.
I sop up the moisture
that makes you slick.

Other words describe the grasp.
Perhaps flexuous.
Curvy preempts slender in the game of hips.

When poets come together, a chess game.
You prefer to knock my piece off the board
rather than scream checkmate from the bedposts.

It is the curse of verse
made worse by the crime of
rhyme.

I prefer unwavering, you hold on to firm.
A turn of events no reason
to head for the exit.

There are no sliding glass doors in Verona.
Balconies are passive aggressive --
just say you want to be on top.

Lover

Electra was on me all the time
convinced I stole her thunder.
I let her finish.
Everything went back to childhood.
She was off the hook about mother
cutting her off.
"I'm a Boy!"
I loved her just the same, great gal.
Devoted to pleasing me.
Never satisfied.
Played the table quite adroitly.
All her drawers were interchangeable.
What was there not to like!
I wanted to follow her footsteps
but I was already there
before her.
I desired a lock of hair.
Afraid to ask
I left her mine at the grave
where she lured us all.
Paybacks are hell.

__Baptism__

In the 1990's, thousands of trees were pulled
from the bottom of Lake Superior
and converted into violins, drums, and guitars.

The cold water altered fibers in the
wood giving added resonance
to acoustic instruments.

When the Pope banned women
from public singing in the mid-16th century,
young men were castrated to fill the void.

When I was ten, I would lie
on the bottom of my grandfather's pool
and think about pretty girls.

At sixteen, a friend of mine found God.
She submerged herself in ritual
and began singing in the chorus at school.

Her older sister drove the three of us to
a place called Nicodemus where we dropped
acid, took off our clothes, swam naked.

After the christening, the older sister
took to singing a different tune
in her bedroom.

She called me to her chambers
and guided my fingers into
her dark Spanish mouth.

She said I looked like Jesus.

Bookends

I met Sylvie A. when I was twelve.
She stood waist-deep in the lull between the waves.
Magnificent above the foam.

The reflection off the water enunciated her brown skin
Bonjour fleshing-out the appropriate words
from my dad on shore.

"Voulez-vous faire une promenade?"
"Oui."
So, walk we did: up and down the beach holding hands;
a kiss on both cheeks, then running
on those long legs all the way back to Quebec.

We wrote letters and vowed to marry
until puberty and 1,000 miles pulled us
in different directions.

My father died.

Then I met Sylvie B. in a bookstore, on a shelf.
She called to me from a pink mouth.
Her slant and style angled into my mind.

The hardback against my sweaty palms,
seeking a line, a refrain, to crack her spine.

I looked around to make sure no one saw the words
that gave me paws:
heard me breathing through my mask; or witnessed
the heat distilling from delicious sin.

I had every intention of paying for her translucency.

<u>Neophyte</u>

And on the seventh day, God nailed her.
He did not rest. Nor did I.
He saw me gape and worship at the window
and in anger laid down the gauntlet:
"You can be poet or lover but not both!"

But you cut your teeth on lesser gods.

Zeus ran screaming from your house:
"S.O.S. Lover in distress!"
Held captive for three ovulating days.
His thunder and lightning extinguished by your hips.

Icarus flew too close to the circle of light
then drowned in your liquid sea.
Daedalus made blueprints of the labyrinth to your soul,
fled to Egypt, and became a god.

Bearing the gift of flattery and truth, my allusion –
"Never have I read an epic more honest in praise
of a woman's mind!"

From your mouth to my comeuppance:
"I levitate above you, the sound of glitter
in the ears I hold."

Do not purge the poet who
burns for the wild hairs of your song.

"Take from me as you see fit
and fit you will most perfectly.
Enter master, leave as slave
bound forever inside of me."

<u>Jam</u>

I have pined for six days, six unholy days in trance,
           to the goddess, sole queen in the soul palace
           of prose-rock, the underground séance for
           the corroborators of lyric, of mayhem,
           of lust and fear,
Purged from the blues that eat away at my mind, the
           voyeur forgotten in the wings, unable to fly
           or rest in the birdcage by bedrooms, by
           baths, by keyboards typing the insinuations
           of jazz and stamen philosophy where God
           penetrates all,
In the revelation of the moment, loving dirty or not at all
           because poetry speaks to a new generation,
           speaks to women who throttle, punch, and
           beat their way through roadblocks that elicit
           the screams of mayday and distress.

II.

What possessed you to write without endings or detours
           exploring the rhythm of the improvised
           mind; the jazz and feminine flush
           of extension in a country of liberal
           openings and pink longings by which you
           erect your stature?

What possessed you to plead for the filth, the unholy,
           the brutal master, not grateful for the soul
           his cock tickles?

What possessed you to want to be possessed?
             not be hollow? to hide behind slave to
             become master? vengeance? past wrongs?
             the smack of daddy? someone pissing on the
             gold-laced wings of the heroine?

III.

I have not seen you pass through the corridors or through
             the halls or heard you breathing from under
             the floor boards or in the attic, the haunt and
             tease of the wind at my back,

Help me to understand the nature of what makes you tick,
             the contrapuntal clock that strikes against me,
             without gears, without hands, without seconds
             to spare for the sufferers of lack, will, and
             boundaries?

Do you speak in a voice unpretentious soft and silky?
             sultry like the summer nights in fields
             of long grass where lovers lie with backs
             to the garden who in spasms of pain break
             the spell of the unattainable?

Are you happy now? do you smile? Is your smile crook?
             like a bead of sweat slithering down
             your thighs between everything that sucks
             me in, your talent immeasurable beyond the
             folds of pleated sycophants and the creases
             on every overturned page.

I worried about you to a point of distraction, then fear
            and anxiety took over and I thought you
            dead, gone from the communicable disease
            of the heart, and the congenital lovers you
            have crucified, to the tissue and substance
            that I wish I had dissected before.

Mantra

I smile
      because beneath their strings
lies a trembling loss of will.

The Senses Five

Aside: (In my talk with the senses five
I was fortunate enough to get each
of them to openly discuss their niche
approach on how best to keep love alive.)

Sight spoke of the eyes and what they portend:
"to be or not to behave." **Smell** chimed in,
"No! Scent is the spice, the essence within,
for which every push and pull depends."

"Have you not heard of music to the ears?"
Sound roared! "Take me please" leaves men short of breath.
But **Touch** disagreed, "These hands know the depth
of longing; where each finger disappears."

Said **Taste**, "ignore all this hullabaloo,
imagine what I get to suck up to."

Synesthesia

Monday is blue.
  Tuesday red.
Wednesday is gray.
  Thursday purple.
Friday is orange.
  Saturday yellow and
Sunday green.

The Russian composer Alexander Scriabin
had *Synesthesia,* a condition
where two or more senses intertwine.
He heard music as colors.

I had *Calendar Synesthesia.*
The days of the week had corresponding colors.
Each month a different hue appeared in circular form.

When I tripped out, I would lie on my back
and put a clear prism ashtray over my right eye
while listening to *Magical Mystery Tour.*

I had a Sansui Reverberation unit
that gave a color coordinated
interpretation to every song based on the degree of echo.

I told Penelope we could only
make love on Tuesday red or purple Thursday
because they were my passionate days.

Fortunately, Penelope was a fellow *Synesthete*
sensitive in every part of her body.
Her specialty was auditory-tactile.

While she practiced CPR
I began working on the back of her neck.
Queen's "A Day at the Races" was in spin.

She preferred I take my time.

Witch Hunt

I first met her behind
a Salem menthol.

I offered her a light.

But she flicked me off
drawing a shiny silver Zippo
with the distinctive click
from the pocket of her well-worn black robe.

The city was on fire.
Saturday night feeding into Sunday morn, Sabbat.
The intersection of Suspicion and Resentment.
2am last call.

A street corner hopping.
Cross-walkers against the traffic
Cross-dressers hitting the after-hours clubs
couples angling
loners heading home
bums meditating and
witches a-brew.

There she stood,
disarming my soul
with contortions and screams.

I suggested Italian be her last.
She declined.
"Svelte doesn't happen by itself, love!"

She hung around.
Apostasy wore her resistance
down.

The kiss of shame
under the street light
now surrendering to dawn.

The Salem came out
along with the attitude
and the silver Zippo.

Projections From a Car

It used to be fun to drive.

GTO. Cobra. Barracuda.
No space between the rubber
and the road.

Personification and kicks.
"What's she got under the hood?"
"How fast can she go?"

Wheels rotated on their axis.
Girls revolved around the sun.
The rumble and science of love.

I drove. She navigated.

On the back roads
across the vertebrae of chance.
Top down, stars aligned.

The O-meter moved in
tandem with the wind
tactile through our hair.

Radio merged with need.
I yielded to the sounds that
accelerated the beat of my heart.

Our parts worn.

Her habit turned gray.
The ritual once familiar
she now shelters like a nun.

The prophylactics of pistons and valves.
The mechanics of going down the same road.
Our secrets undercover in the garage.

I hear McQueen rev his Mustang.
Popeye Doyle floors it through Brooklyn.
And I slip into compromise for a rehabilitative walk.

It used to be fun to drive.

The Girl Who Thought She Was Wild

There were no clandestine meetings with her alter ego.
No parades of softness for the plebeians.
The psycho-swamis heard no confessions about a Barbie beheading.
She was not cruel to animals.

In teenage summer she ran with the boys.
There was no perfume in her sweat.
She smelled of adolescence and things untouched.

To the girls she was standoffish, shy.
Seances of slander and drama never held her captive.
She read Jane Austen and D.H. Lawrence.
No revelations there.

Music failed to move her
nor did nostalgia tender her heart.
She was moved by only one thing:
the onset and flush of wildness.

At seventeen the crushing desire began.
Exhilaration swam through her vanity.
Questioning turned to answering the doorbell late at night.

A narcissist dressed her down.
I rescued her from a laptop.
Shared my townhouse, a Siamese, and an understanding.

We came from the same place but danced under a different moon.
I practiced lonely in a bedroom below.
She took up painting and stroked anonymous women.

Sunset

She was on the roof.
Channeling with bowl and spoon.
I was trespassing like an M.R.I.

I interrupted her intimacy.
From the ground up.
Comments about perspective.

I was older than the sunset.
In her eyes
not on the same level.

She availed herself to the stars.
Perhaps her studies pushed her.
Passion and nutrition unfulfilled.

Pretty twenty does not know from sunset or
walking down the lonely corridor.
Sunrise awakening is her gig.

But there she was, alone.
A story above my poem.
Trumping me in all natural fields of engagement.

Primates drag close to the earth.
Our evolution strains the imagination.
We dream in verbs: Jump. Fall. Catch.

Love thy neighbor.
Bathe in her youth.
Tomorrow my shingles shot.

<u>Snow Blind</u>

I was a bluish-purple
weathercock vein and fury
curved over the sofa where she
presented her slippery

will like Lara to her Zhivago;
an apparition across her threshold
opening doors cupboards lips

after ice-encrusted Levi's
fell below my knees from
the chattering teeth of heavy metal

unzipped for an icicle seeking warmth
melting into dumb unison
"O My God, O My God!!"

My reward for the effort
of trudging 6-miles bootstrapped
gloved and sheathed from toe to
crown through the wild of a

January night.

<u>Jam</u>

I met Klara in Berlin at Tier Garten Park. It was a gorgeous day and I wanted to take some photographs of people walking about and their reactions to the first days of spring. Klara was painting a young woman sitting alone beside a

lake surrounded by trees and daffodils. I struck up a conversation and discovered we both lived on the sixth floor in the same apartment building. She seemed to me rather shy. One day Klara knocked on my apartment door and asked if I

would photograph her. I told her my preference was outdoor nature scenes where in black and white I could portray the coldness and alienation of passersby, loners, misfits, and the homeless. She understood my artistic preferences but wanted

my expertise, as she put it, and offered to pay me two-hundred Euros for my efforts. She recently moved here from India and did not know anyone with a video camera which upon reflection was more than likely the impetus that led her

to my door. Klara was an attractive girl in her twenties who lived alone like me and had few friends. Every time I saw her getting on and off the lift, or entering or exiting the building, she was always by herself. She did not say who

the video was for other than it was a gift for a friend. I agreed and brought my video camera and tripod over the next day. Her apartment had plenty of natural light. It was a bright sunny day. And so, we began. Klara sat in front of a

large window in an alcove off the living room. Her back was
against the wall and her outstretched legs formed a ninety-
degree angle. The Berlin traffic droned six stories below. She
had just bathed and smelled of lavender. Her thick black hair

tied from behind highlighted her pretty face. Klara had large
dark eyes. Her nose was straight and thick. Her lips appeared
soft as did her skin. She took pencil to pad and began
sketching a girl; perhaps someone she missed, pined for,

once loved or was now the object of her affection. The face
and hair were easy for her to draw and instantly took shape.
The girl bedecked with jewels, donned the sari of her native
land. But beyond the girl's slender shoulders Klara drew a blank.

Frustrated by the lack of precision the medium proscribed,
she paused, then put the pencil and paper down. Klara moved
from the alcove and sat cross-legged against the wall. There was
a small lamp to her left. I followed her with my camera

preferring to let her improvise as she saw fit. She obviously
felt something more real, more personal, because she untied
her hair and let it fall. She stood up and took off all her clothes.
There was no striptease or drama in her movements. Then she

sat back down on the floor and began playing with herself.
I remained focused on her face. Her eyes closed and she
gently bit her upper lip. I said nothing and continued to
photograph her as was her wish.

But as Klara delved deeper into herself, I became self-
conscious and confused. When she came, I left. This scenario
played out for the next several days. She began by drawing
the same girl, struck a meditative pose on the floor, stood up,

removed her clothes, and fingered herself until she climaxed.
She said nothing and neither did I. I left each time after she
was satisfied. Her smile. My goodbye. On the fourth day,
Klara's ecstasy hit a fevered pitch. With her head cocked back

and her large oval eyes looking upward, she uttered the name
'Mira' as all tension left her body. I could stand it no more. I
asked who Mira was and why she wanted me here photographing
her in what should be a private matter. Klara said:

*Friend, I long for the rain when saint Mira will return to me. I
wait every day for her to come back. She is my one true love.
I give myself only to her. I have no other lovers. The picture I
draw is her, as I recall. At the mere sight of her I become like*

*water. She flows into me and I flow into her. You are the conduit
for which our love is bound. The video is my gift to Mira. I only
hope that I am worthy of her affection. My arms, my heart, my bed
are empty without her. I know no other love.*

The following day I returned to Klara's apartment. She opened
the door only halfway making it clear she wanted me to remain
in the hallway. She was in a state of euphoria and revealed
to me Mira's return.

*Friend, the rains have come today and cleansed me of
my impatience and insecurity. Mira has come back and my body
now opens to her. I am here to please only her and this I must
do alone for our love is sublime.*

Klara paid me in full. I handed her the video tape I had recorded.
"Namaste" came from the lips that now quivered in delight.
She bowed her head. I thanked her and went back to
my apartment. I became a well-respected man.

Mantra

I smile
      because the act of creation
brings me that much closer to God.

Erato

The greatest of all amusements!
    Insurmountable stairway to the stars.
I envy the introspection of your eyes.

Propose we meet on the horizon
    beyond the eclipse of sail and sun;
midnight on a Venusian cloud
    where I can levitate your senses.
From the surface of your flesh
    I will paint the crepuscular sky.
My kiss, the signature on a masterpiece.

When the earth moves again
    turn to me, my exquisite Muse,
And I will lick you like a thousand suns.

No Admittance

I wear my pants on the outside.
I bleed vanilla.
I am a smooth stone from Eilat.

It may have been Studio 54.
The Wave in Arizona.
A date with Joan of Arc.

I kept my appointment with her eyes.
At 12 AM the clock struck 11.
In bed with the moon.

Defined by the proper letters,
no one questioned her.
Front row seats at the chimera.

Erotica from the sapped.
Clay feet in Versace pumps.
The gatekeeper let her in.

I read the eulogy at Sisyphus' funeral.
Skimmed stones across The Lost Star.
The back of the line my rock.

<u>Lack</u>

Danu works at the donation center
and checks the pockets of every pair of pants
that walks in the store.
She found a leprechaun in a Versace suit.

Post-op from my appendectomy
Erasmus left me a zippered scar so
I could look into my soul.

Under the rubric of improvisation
my date recited these lines
before she hid in my nightmare:

Disarm the madman,
    waver the tempo of his strike
Supplant his fire with mine
    I, the keeper of the pulse.
Thou shall know thy rage
    When my seething yields to force
Ne'er shall I bend to love
    Nor tempest suffice.

Unlike her, you are not
afraid to put your honey-where your mouth is.
"The fresh voice of a new chapter!"
I am quite comfortable.

I want for nothing.

<u>Poet</u>

I do not know what to do
with poetry once
I write it.

I watch my cat in the loo
covering up his afterword.
Sand in the gears of critics.

My publisher sends my books
to Amazon and places beyond
the mouth of the great river.

I read that everyone writes poetry
but nobody reads it.
Bookshelves full of eager lovers.

In dreams there is often an eclipse.
One face turns into another.
A spoon appears bent in a glass of water.

Van Gogh cut off his ear
and gave it to a cleaning-woman at a brothel.
She fainted when she uncovered it.

His paintings had not been selling well.
He resorted to an old poetic trick.
He saw someone he wanted her to be.

My muse sent me a lock of her hair.
I greedily brought the strands to my nose.
Poets are so predictable.

The Sun is a Lonely Girl

I have stared at you for far too long
defied the gods and Hippocratic oath (the addendum)
to look away as any lay person should.

I have tanned under your spotlight
in preparation for the weekend orgy
of dance floors and horizontal leanings
only to have the mania of vitamin D
keep me unprotected from the bewitching spell of night.

I have forsaken the star of David
in awe of your power and promise of warmth.

I was there when you slow danced with the moon
and shed darkness and anxiety to our fore-bearers
that saw your mystery as the omnipresence of God.

When I designed my exodus to the equator
and loosened the belt around his waist
you advised me to remain lenient
on a lounge chair, secure in my latitude.

When you lightened my hair, the girls revolved –
I thank you for that
along with the darkened skin that covered my flaws.

You never age – I do!
And what will become of the grass on my grave
where once I danced in your glory?

Why do you stimulate, then take it away?

I have chlorophyll in my veins –
tilt my head like a sunflower when you speak.

All the stars are suns.
There is a multitude of gods.
Night just the blasphemy of day.

<u>Immortality</u>

I wish I could give every cat immortality!
No feline need, ever die.

Litter boxes litter the highway.
Why did kitty cross the road?
No dog tags.

Stand-up bassist.
Black lace boots, tight jeans, leather paws.
The coolest kitten in the room.

She pulls the strings, threads the needle.
She leaves her for a drummer.
Tough break.

You were my pet.
The door always open.
I never kept you from the things you loved.

The purge of the undesirables.
Waning. Waxing.
All the way to the moon.

The resurrection!
Give me fur or give me death!
I wish I could give every cat immortality!

<u>Jam</u>

I saw her tattered, tethered to the wind
Before the current pushed her from behind
And held her up against a wall of air:
She breathed in pure, and pure was her fire.
A dark gray morning, the wind off the shore,
Granted me a sly and slippery pleasure:
My mind unhinged by the outline of clothes;
The tightness of petals curled around a rose.

For her, the stage was neither bad nor good
She knew nothing of the heat of my blood.
Black hair, white sand, she stood before the sun
A sliver set sail with hound running on.
I had but a blink of an eye to choose
Whether to speak or stay silent and lose
This gift of lovely thrown to me by chance.
Does love become known by merely one glance?

My voice cried out, "Yes!" The hound came to me
And sniffed me out with canine chivalry.
The owner sat down and gave me her hand
Put arms around knees and toes in the sand.
We moved from eye to eye, to scent, and trust
I wished her sidekick would leave us to lust.
But there he remained, despite my advice
The woman spoke of love, not once, but twice.

Skillful was I like a poet with words
No mouth could be as delightful as hers.
So, I did what her eyes seemed to suggest:
Lips to meet lips and the curve of her neck.

Wave after wave broke her resistance down
To the swell of parts my deft fingers found.
I swam in her eyes, luxuriously
A face to behold, held only by me.

<u>Mantra</u>

I smile
        because peace will come
if I wait and desire less.

I Could be Someone You Never Knew

Never to be.

Never to be again.

I lived for the moment, in the moment.

The second time I missed the turn.

It will not be that easy to write me off.

But I will always listen.

Memory will remind us of what we did not learn.

Forget the pain, remember the pleasure.

Gratitude is past tense.

Greed is good.

I want mine now.

This is going to feel *very* good.

Passing through.

Perpendicular

I have become more bony
that is, to say,
perpendiculars and dead-end streets
make more sense

than in my youth
when my bones rarely
kept to themselves.

When the flesh rose
to the fore and demanded
satisfaction, my fingers

followed suit. But the wrists
that could hammer your keys
with a modicum of
sensuality and grace

now end at every
point of connection.

Mouth

You will hate me!
I am damaged goods.
I can only love you with my mouth.

My new new dentist praised my orifice.
"Your mouth is a perfect shade of pink."
I wanted to return the compliment.

People used to buy a horse
based on the quality of their bite.
When you are near my teeth tingle.

After we pass the gates of lips
and tongue you and I will lock teeth.
The not so tender trap.

The nerve you strike
is not the nerve you desire.
Nor the one you deserve.

I studied under Pygmalion.
You are my Galatea.
I stand on tiptoes to kiss you.
You are above me.

But I can only love you with my mouth.

Longing is a Short Shrift

If merrily she sings
   play her something dark.
When she is serious
   tell her a joke.
If she laughs
   marry her.

<u>What Gratitude Really Is*</u>

A second chance.

To not make the same mistake again.

A parade of birthday-suited opportunities in front of my eyes.

No slippery fingers.

No losing my grip.

Nothing passing through my hands.

Touch.

Lingering touch.

Taste.

Lingering taste.

A stranglehold on life.

The breath.

Timelessness.

Sunny days.

To exit by the same route as I began.

*A reminder not to take for granted what I once had
and now feverishly want again.

Lullaby

No tears between
the pillows nor ice around
the heart. Our covenant is

Biblical. Had I been Moses
on the mount with you
dancing half-naked
around the golden calf no

commandments would have
made me hang ten. Burning bush?
Yours is the only one
for me baby! Let's play
the second act of

Adam and Eve. You, laughter --
me, hi jinx --
two peas in a bohemian

pod. Nary a cross word
to crucify our faith in
love and fun.

Jam

I waited until a warm sunny spring day, an exemplary day
to compose a letter unlike those summer camp grievances
from barracks, cot by the front door, awful food, lights out
at 9pm, trumpets at dawn, those letters of homesickness,
whining, pleading to come home, where the boys are, the
girls are, where mingling came easy,

To halcyon days playing baseball, the oppressive heat in waves
off asphalt humbling sticky nights into prepubescent
moonlight, backyards like fingers down the spine and tingle
of imagination running wild to thoughts of the name I knew
nothing about, recumbent on the cusp of innocence looking
out into the wilderness of touching fondling, unknown
movements foreshadowing older games of chance,

The words that never seemed to come except in phrases,
quips, laundry lists and grocery lists, lists, the enemy of
carefree backsliding into beloved rock and roll, the teenage
angst, the elevated status of skirts and free love, turnstiles,
cab rides, subways deep in the bowels of the city away
from the mundane,

The repetitiousness of work where a pretty face meant
something special, a break from the ennui, the grunt and
groan of 9-5, no apologies or guilt or the cancer of wills
disgruntled in the night under sheets, backs to each other,
faces looking at opposite walls wondering, dreaming,

The letter I have written in my head a million times since the
beginning when Eve left her identity and overbite in Adam's
fruit, back when couples stayed together, before cynicism
screwed hipsters into coolness, black, haughty, aloof, the
ephemeral seeking shelter in therapy, psychotropic outreach
under the banner of science and supplication,

A letter of endurance beyond the letter "Z", beyond the staid
Alphabet -- 26 limitations on how I should feel putting together
vowels and consonants, mostly vows, to a new lexicon, new
ideas, new faces, New! not "the more things change the more
they stay the same" philosophy but a philosophy espousing
gratitude, finding Santosha without looking, without effort,

Back when pot-filled dreams made the garden seem
attainable, back when freedom meant flights figurative,
lifting our spirit, applauding, and encouraging creativity,

A letter for you, sentiments for you, happiness for you, love
for you, 'U' the best vowel, the only vowel, the vow never
broken by time, by feud, misunderstanding, sabotage, never
broken in half dragging bodies old-aged, wrinkled, arthritic,
and ready for the heap,

A letter written from immortal hands with none of the
incumbent rules of this new world, the wars, crime, greed,
fears of the unenlightened, soulless anarchists who want
to blow it all up in the name of insignificance or the horror of
being alone,

But a letter linking Us. Ours. Always.

Other Books by the Author

Convoluted Whispers

The Catharsis of Form

Wait Awhile

When All Was Well in Wellwood

Still Well in Wellwood